AUDUBON BIRDS
STAINED GLASS PATTERN BOOK

Carol Krez

DOVER PUBLICATIONS, INC.

New York

Bibliographical Note

Audubon Birds Stained Glass Pattern Book is a new work, first published by Dover Publications, Inc., in 1995.

DOVER *Pictorial Archive* SERIES

This book belongs to the Dover Pictorial Archive Series. You may use the designs and illustrations for graphics and crafts applications, free and without special permission, provided that you include no more than four in the same publication or project. (For permission for additional use, please write to: Permissions Department, Dover Publications, Inc., 180 Varick Street, New York, N.Y. 10014.)

However, republication or reproduction of any illustration by any other graphic service, whether it be in a book or in any other design resource, is strictly prohibited.

Library of Congress Cataloging-in-Publication Data

Krez, Carol.
    Audubon birds stained glass pattern book / Carol Krez.
        p.   cm.
    ISBN 0-486-28625-8 (pbk.)
    1. Glass craft—Patterns. 2. Glass staining and painting—Patterns. 3. Birds in art. I. Title.
TT298.K74   1995
748.5'022'2—dc20
                                        95-1406
                                          CIP

Manufactured in the United States of America
Dover Publications, Inc., 31 East 2nd Street, Mineola, N.Y. 11501

Publisher's Note

These practical design patterns represent 60 of John James Audubon's famous birds translated into the medium of stained glass. All are taken from the artist/ornithologist's *The Birds of America* (1840–1844) and not only feature the subjects in their well-known Audubon poses, but re-create, to the extent practicable in stained glass work, the vegetation with which the birds were originally depicted. As well, the designs are structured so as to suggest the natural markings of each bird. Among the birds to be found herein are the Evening Grosbeak, the Dark-eyed Junco, the Indigo Bunting, the Northern Cardinal, the Cedar Waxwing and the Black-capped Chickadee. All the birds are identified.*

*For the user of this book who wishes to consult Audubon's original artwork, full-color plates of all the birds in this collection are to be found in Dover's *Treasury of Audubon Birds* (0-486-27604-X).

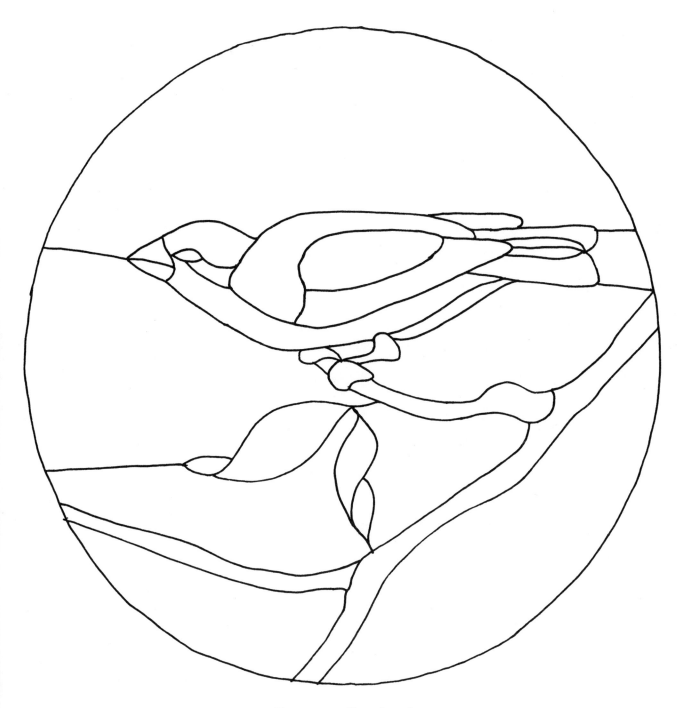

Evening Grosbeak
(Male)

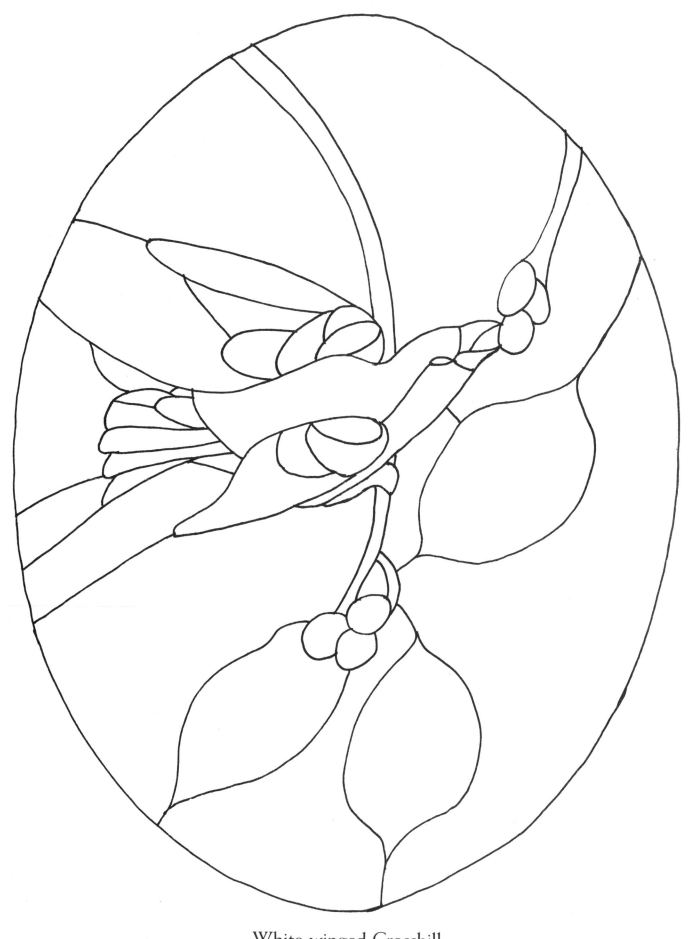

White-winged Crossbill
(Male)

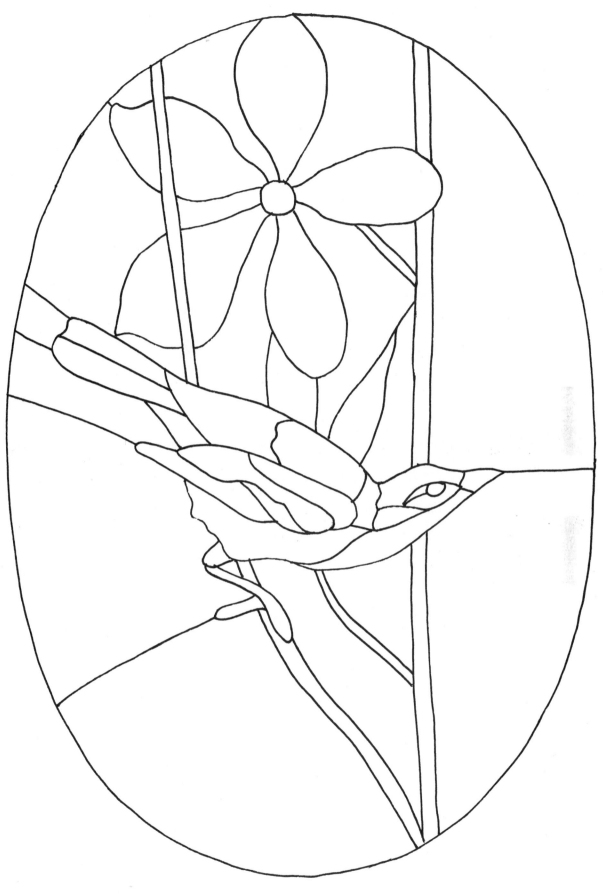

Troupial
(Male)

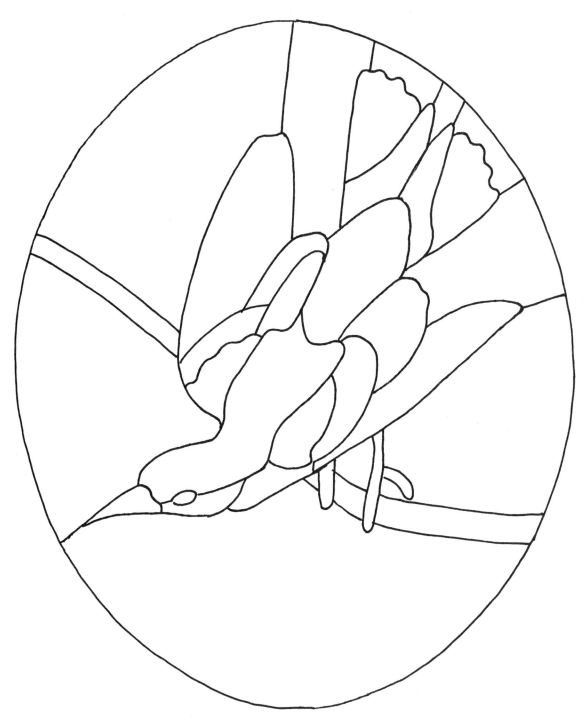

Northern Oriole

(Male)

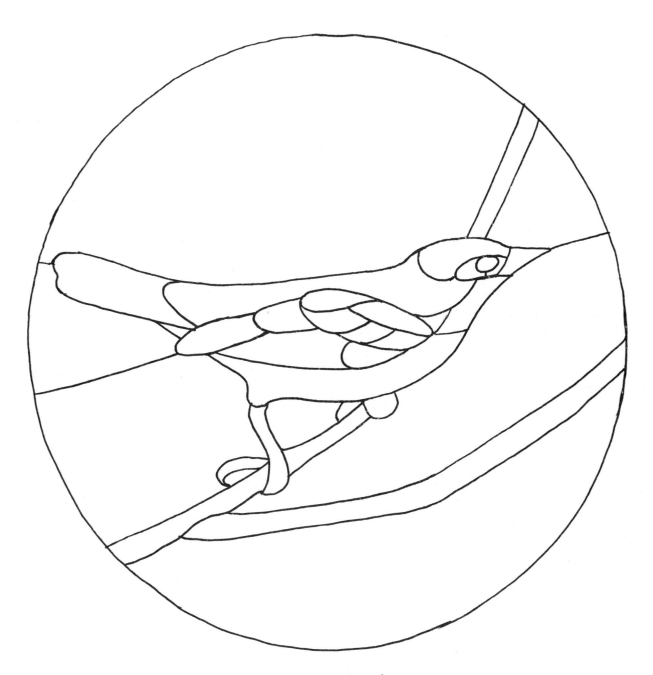

Northern Oriole
(Female)

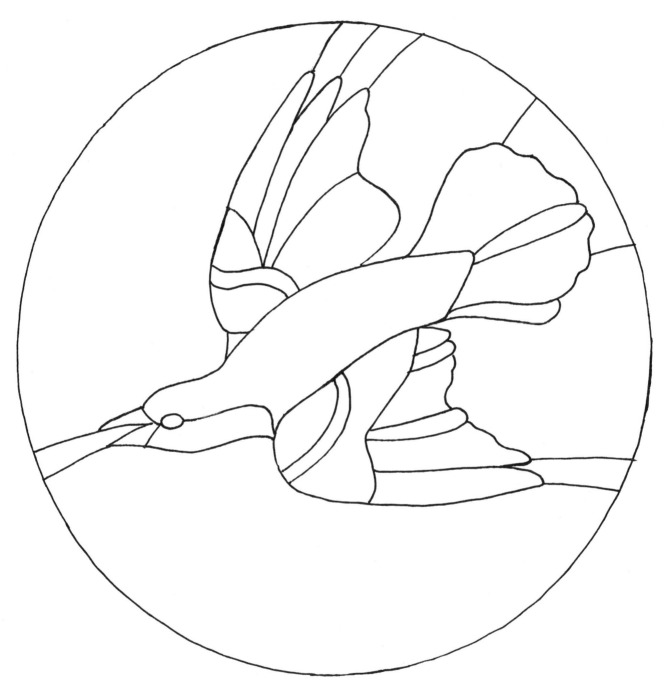

Red-winged Blackbird
(Male)

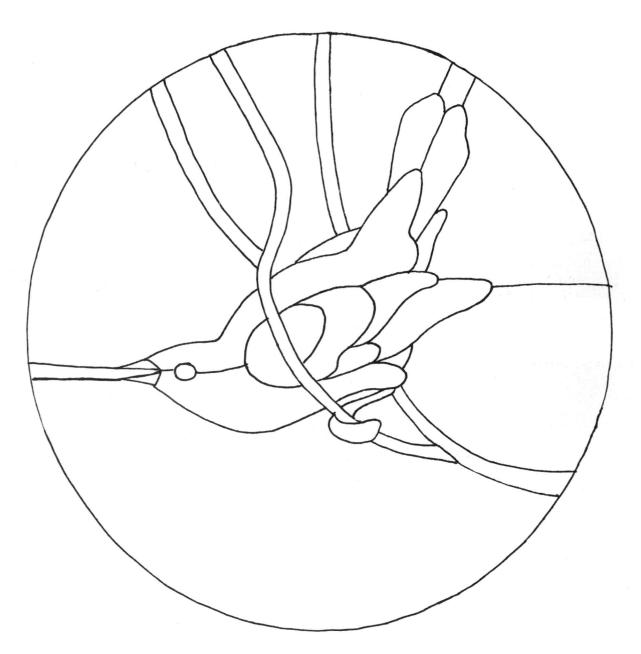

Red-winged Blackbird

(Female)

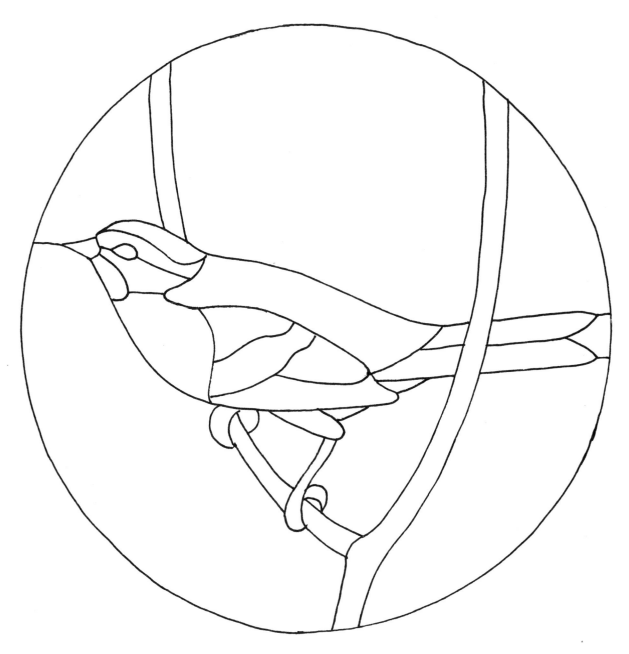

White-throated Sparrow

(Male)

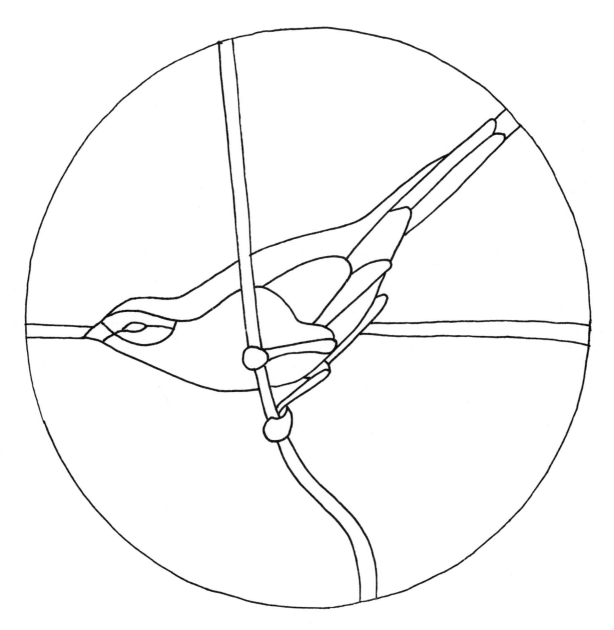

White-throated Sparrow
(Female)

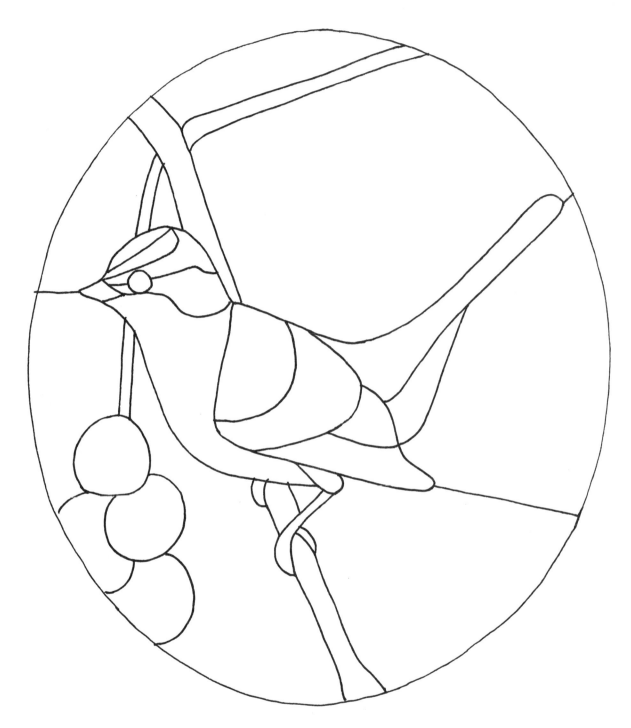

White-crowned Sparrow
(Male)

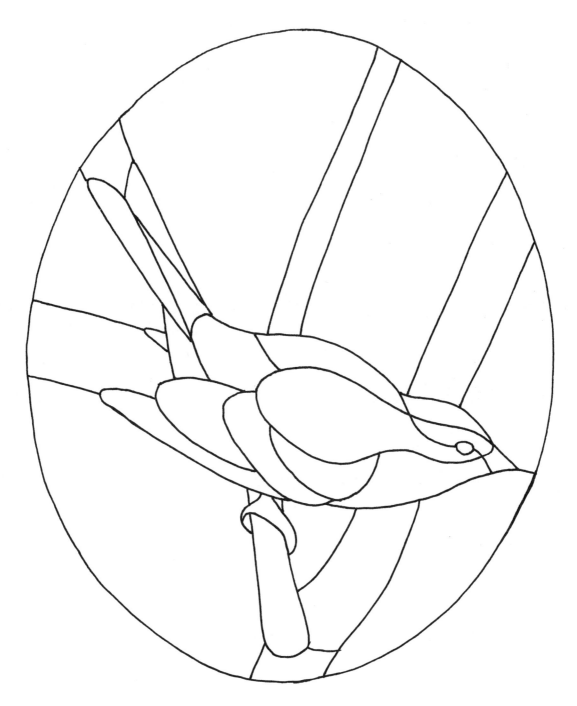

Chipping Sparrow
(Male)

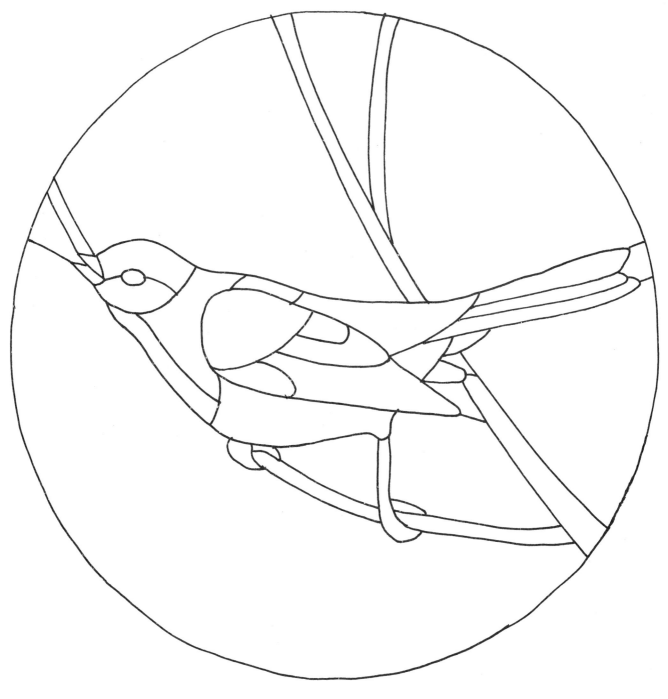

Dark-eyed Junco
(*Male*)

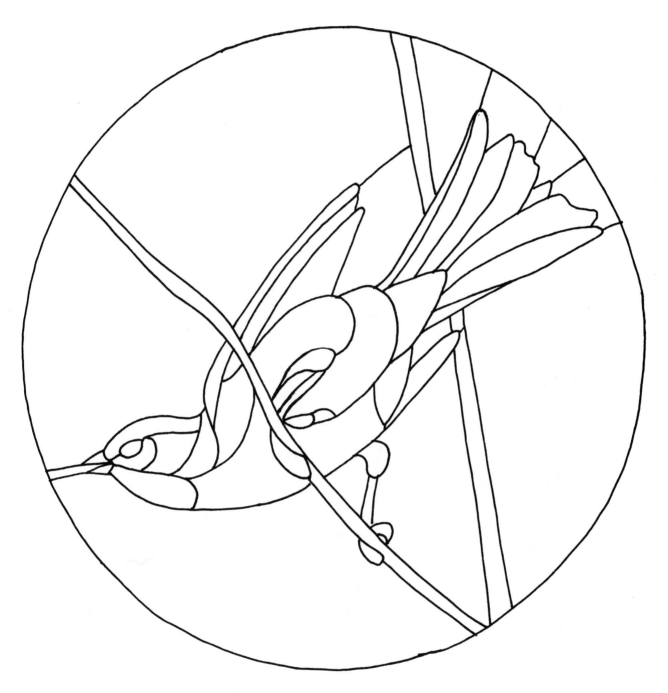

American Tree Sparrow
(*Female*)

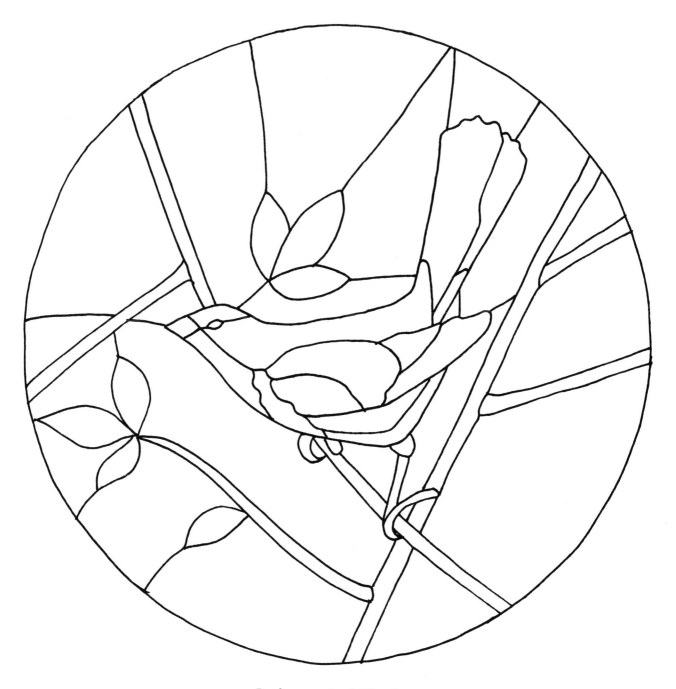

Rufous-sided Towhee

(Male)

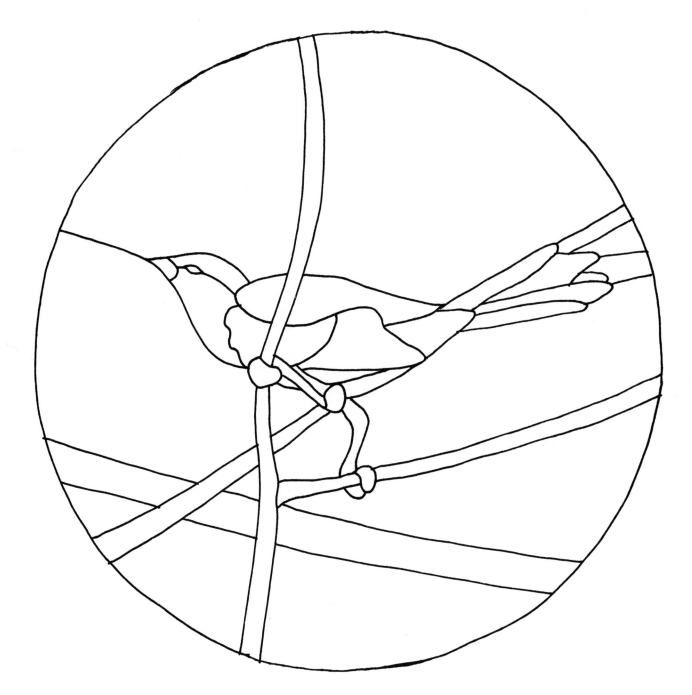

Rufous-sided Towhee
(Female)

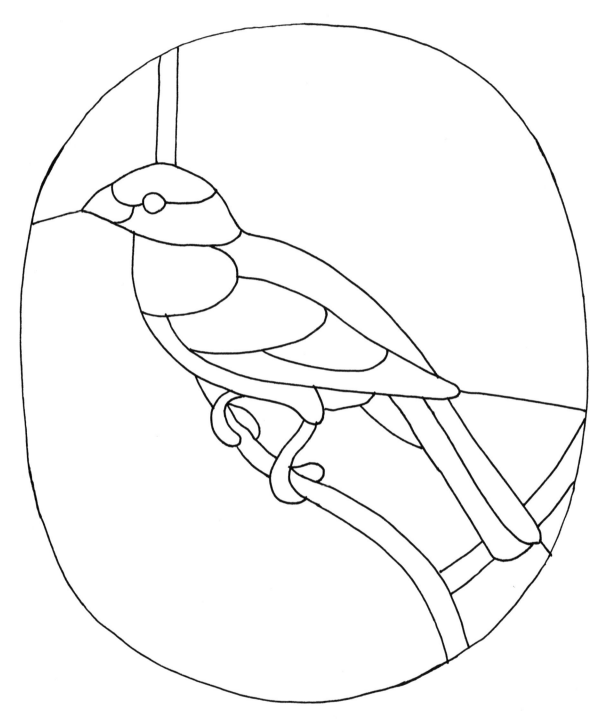

Black-headed Grosbeak
(Male)

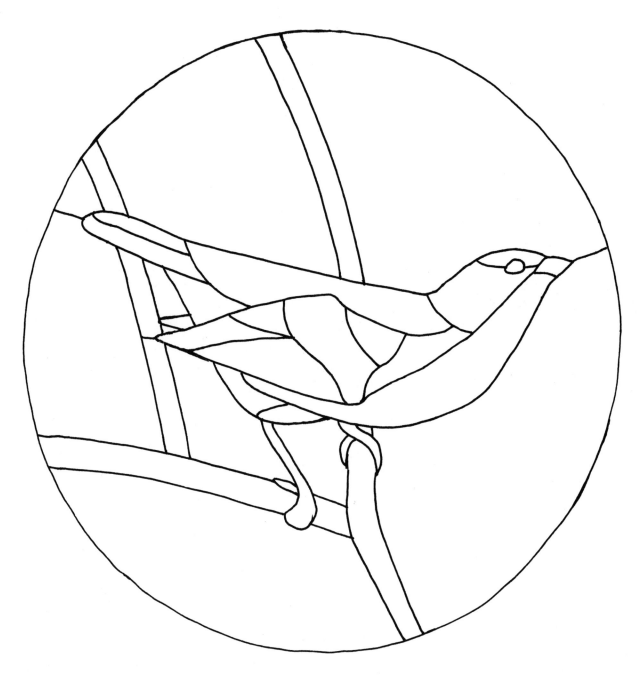

Painted Bunting
(Female)

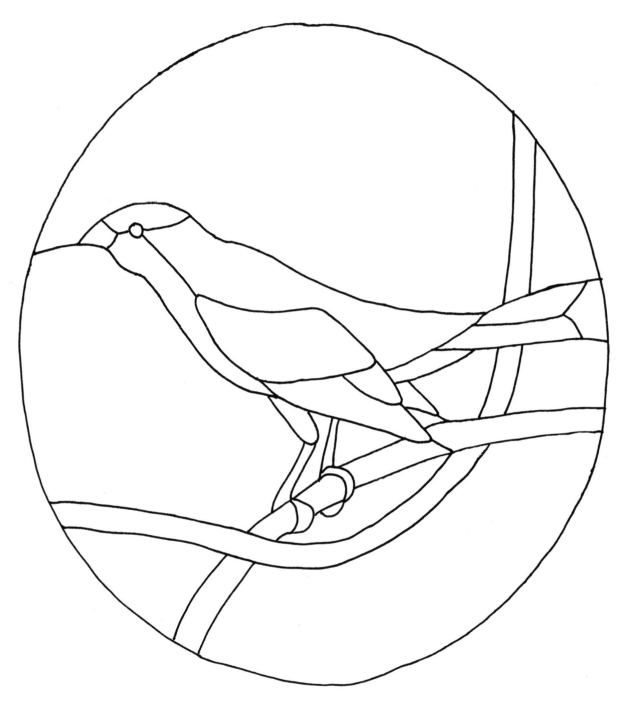

Indigo Bunting
(Male)

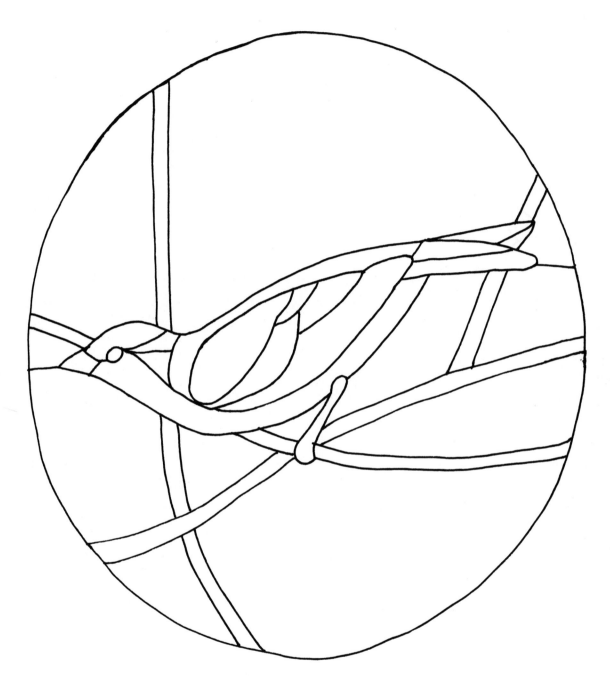

Indigo Bunting
(Male)

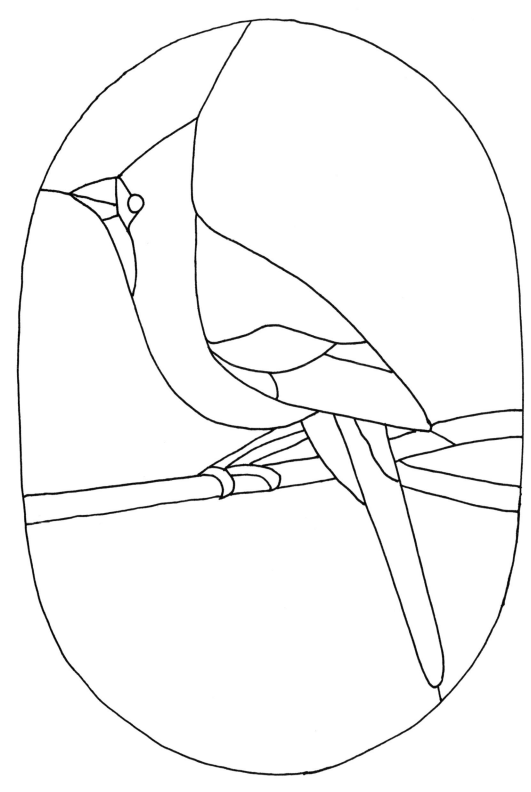

Northern Cardinal
(Male)

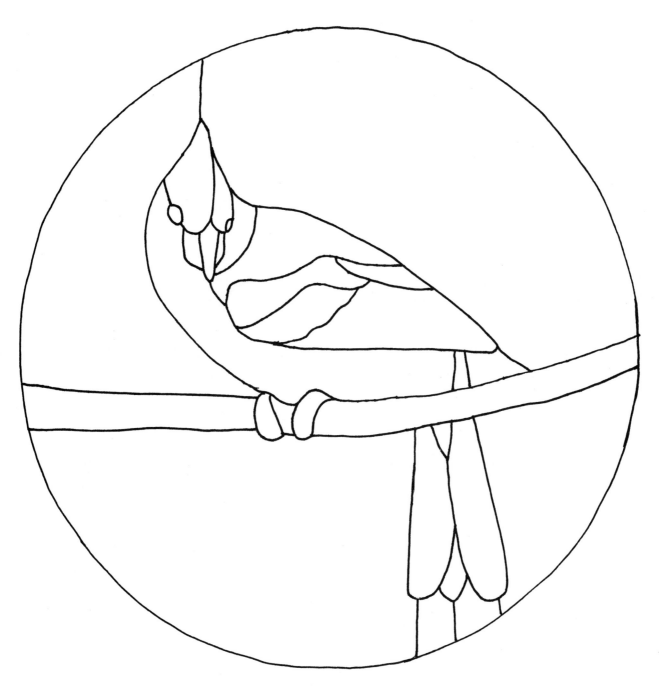

Northern Cardinal
(Female)

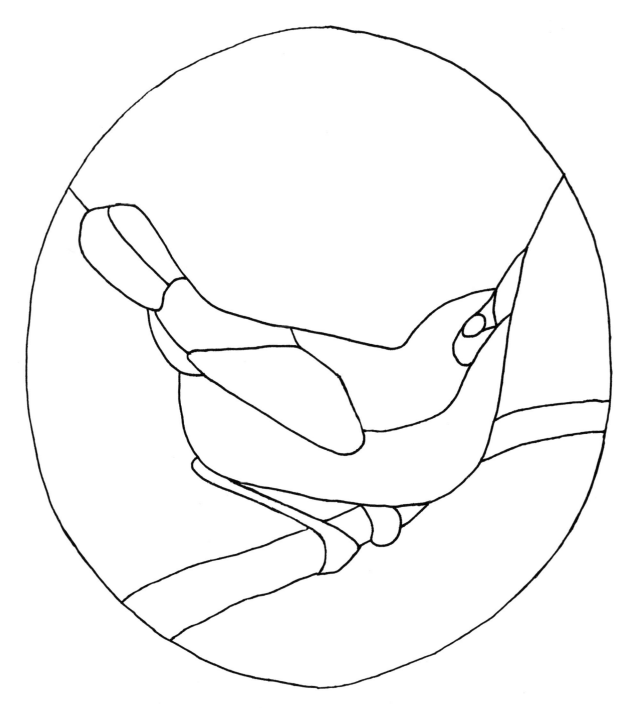

Common Yellowthroat

(Female)

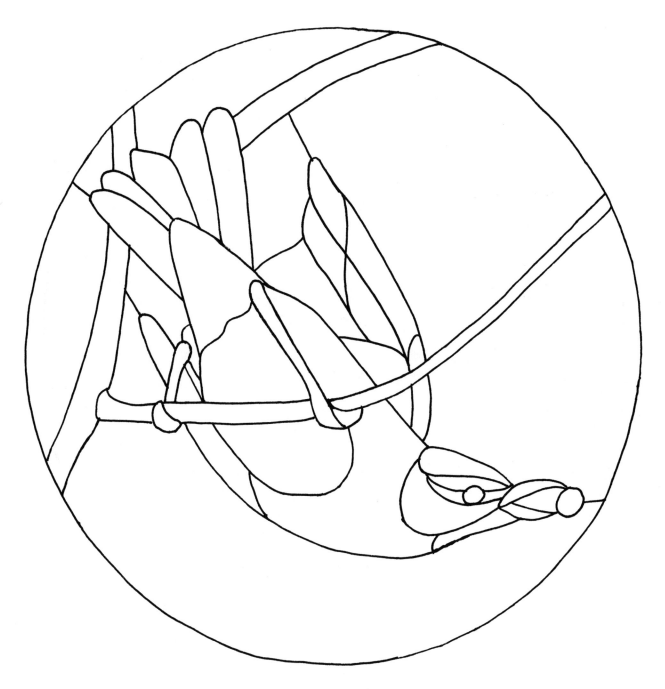

Palm Warbler

(Male)

Yellow Warbler
(Male)

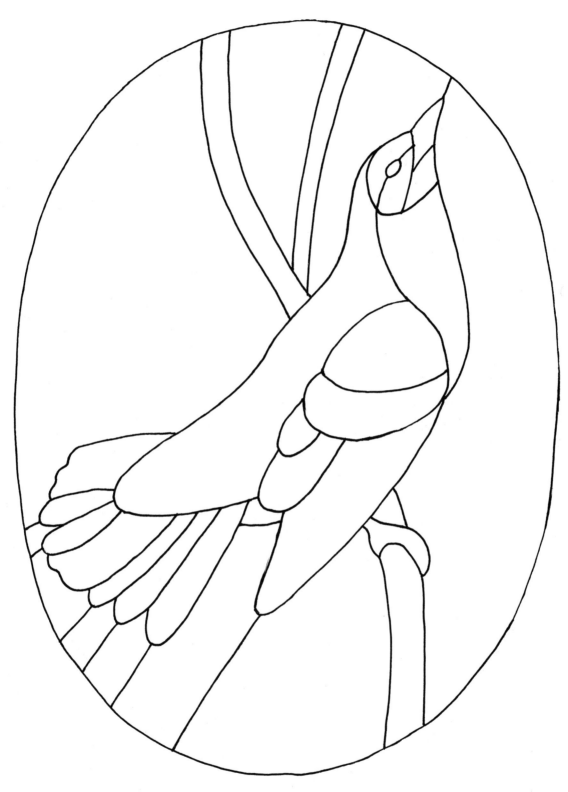

Yellow Warbler
(Male)

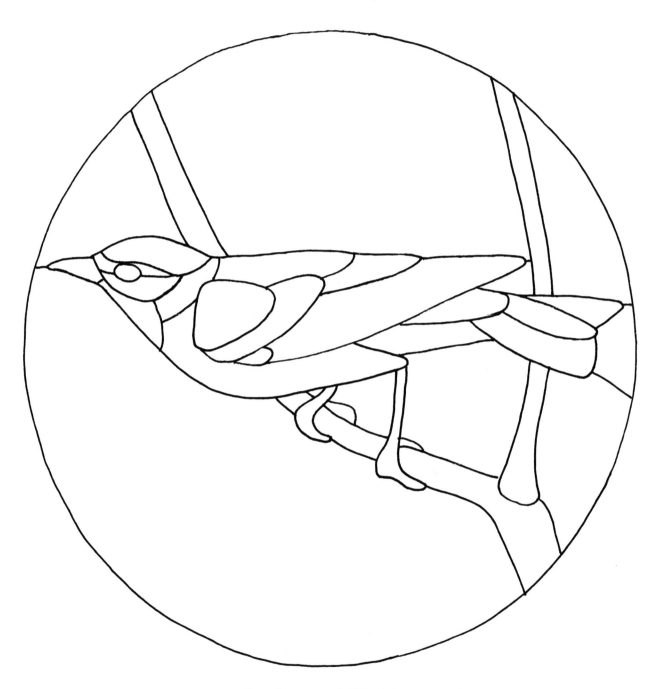

Bay-breasted Warbler
(Male)

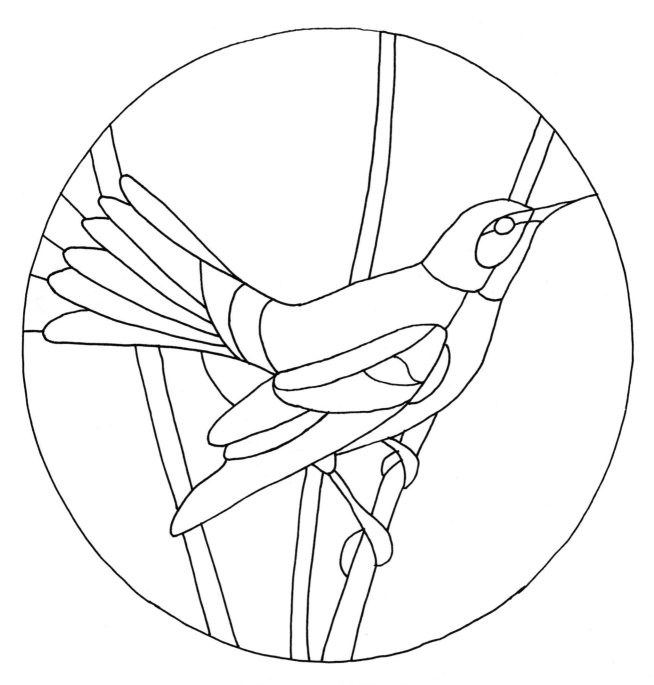

Yellow-rumped Warbler
(*Male*)

Black-throated Green Warbler
(Male)

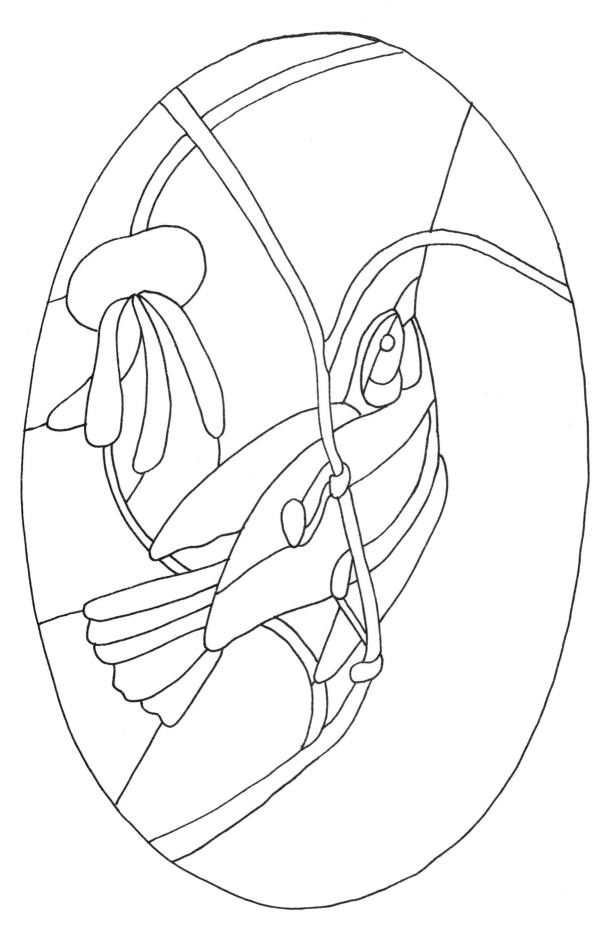

Black-throated Green Warbler

(Female)

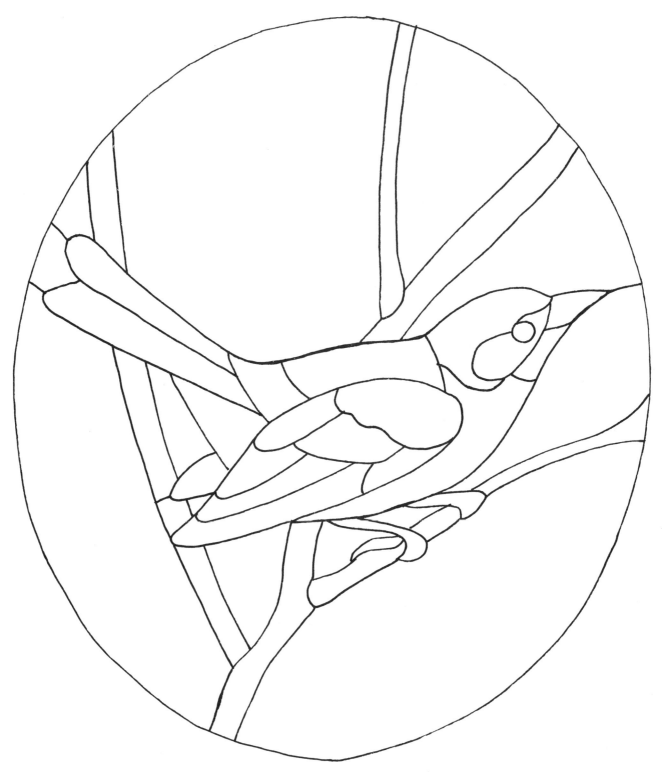

Magnolia Warbler

(*Male*)

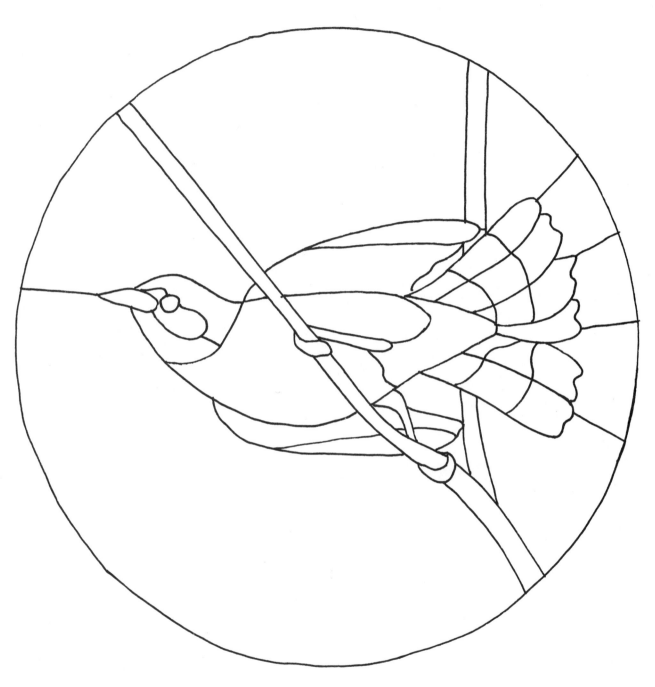

Magnolia Warbler
(Female)

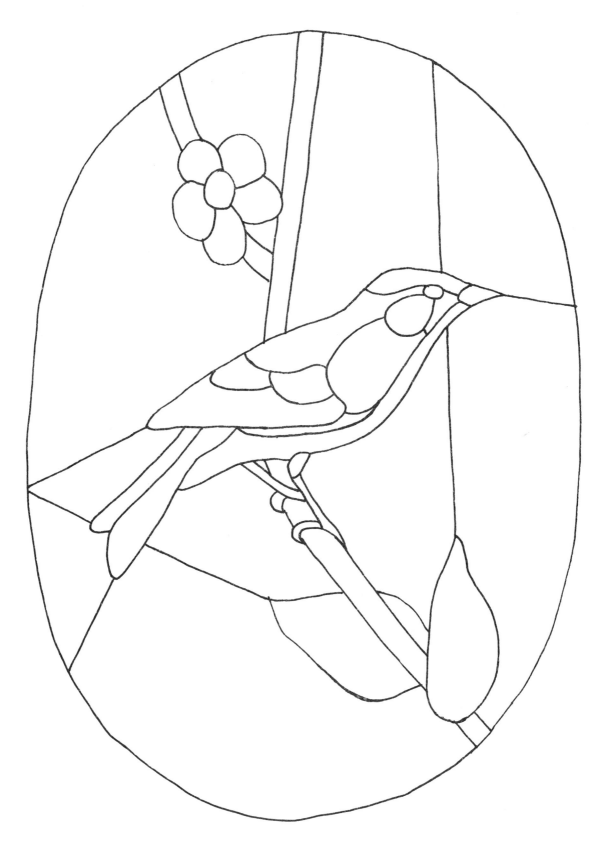

Chestnut-sided Warbler

(Male)

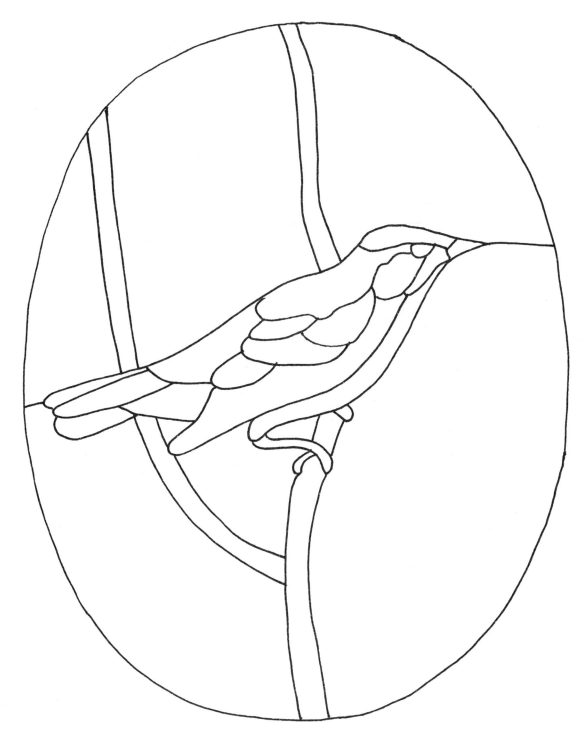

Chestnut-sided Warbler

(Female)

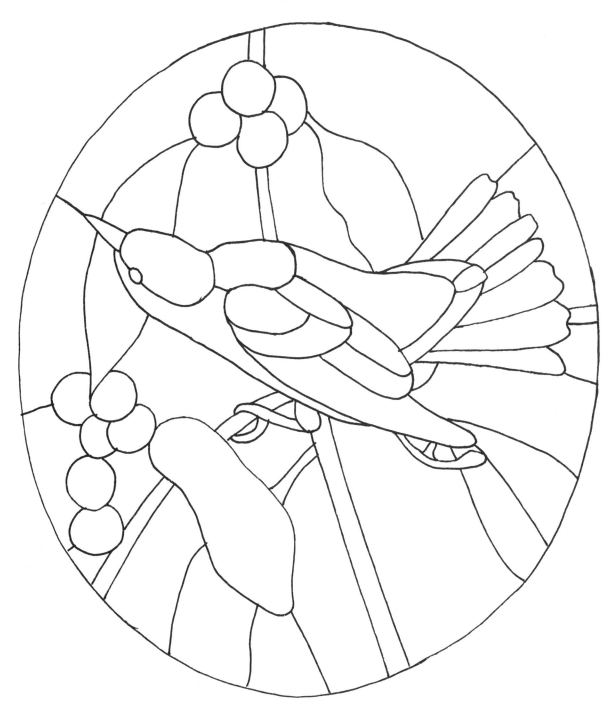

Cerulean Warbler

(Male)

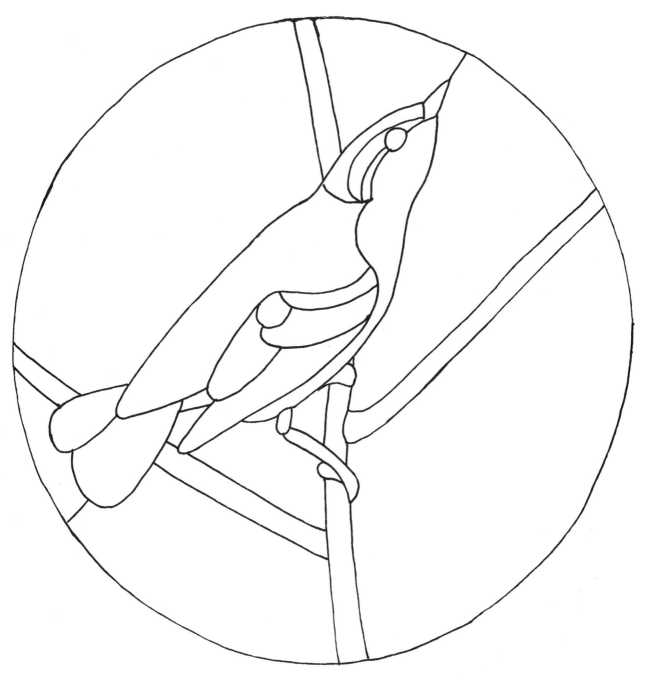

Cerulean Warbler

(Young Male)

Black-throated Blue Warbler

(Male)

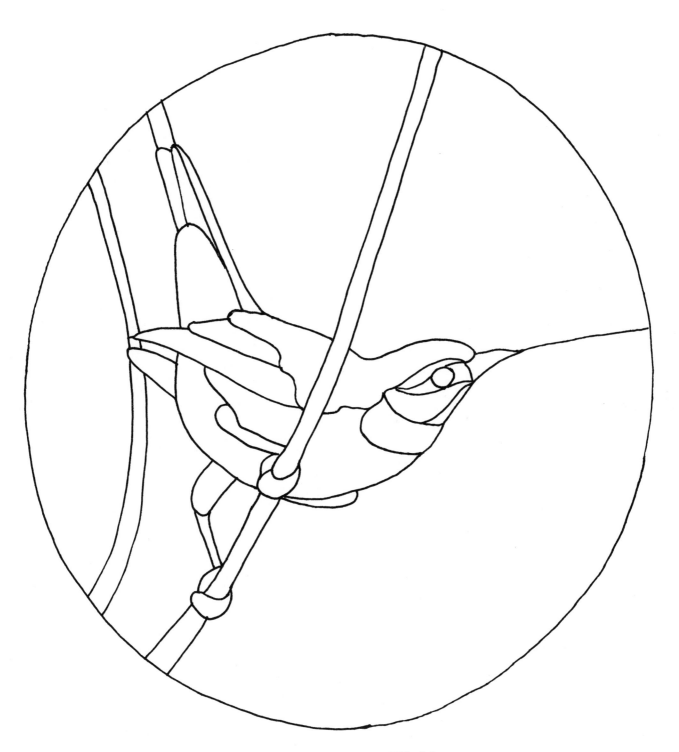

Black-throated Blue Warbler

(Female)

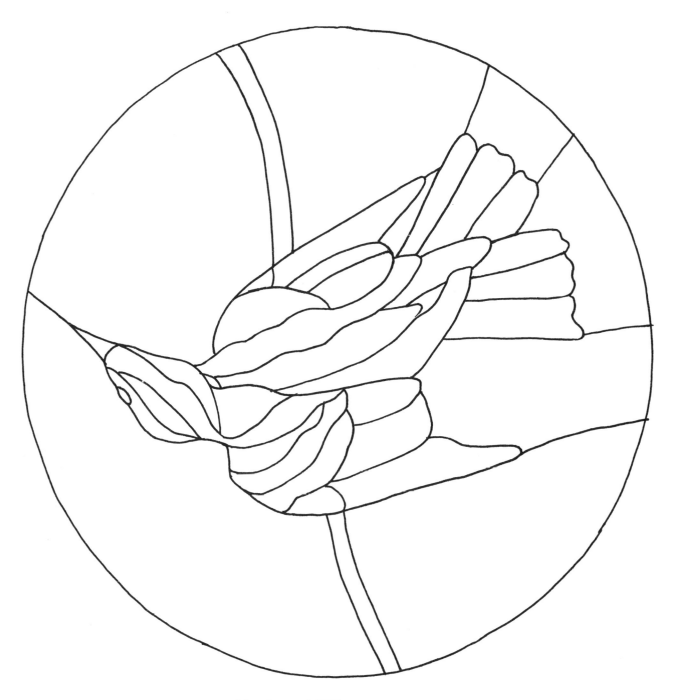

Black-and-White Warbler

(Male)

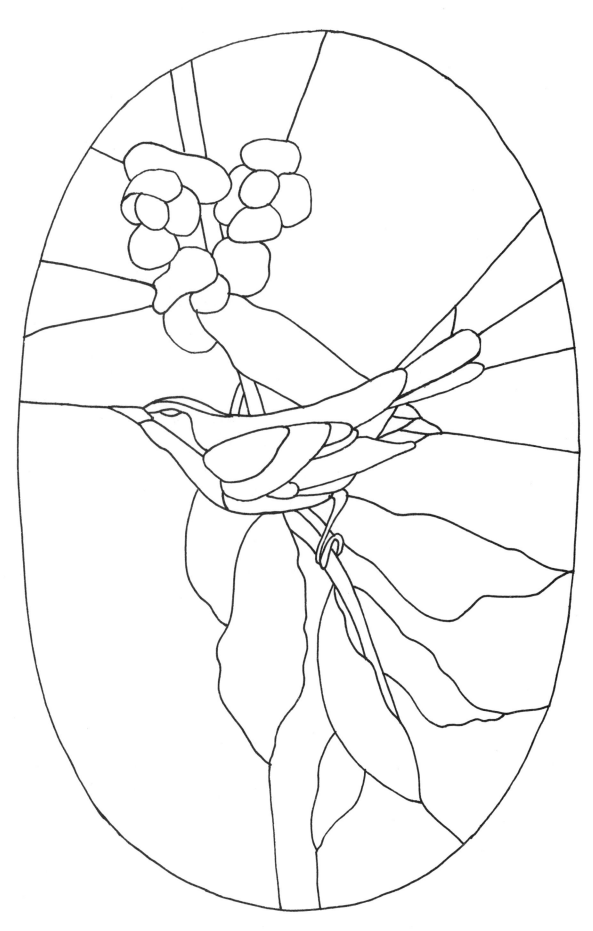

Yellow-throated Warbler

(Male)

Northern Parula
(Male)

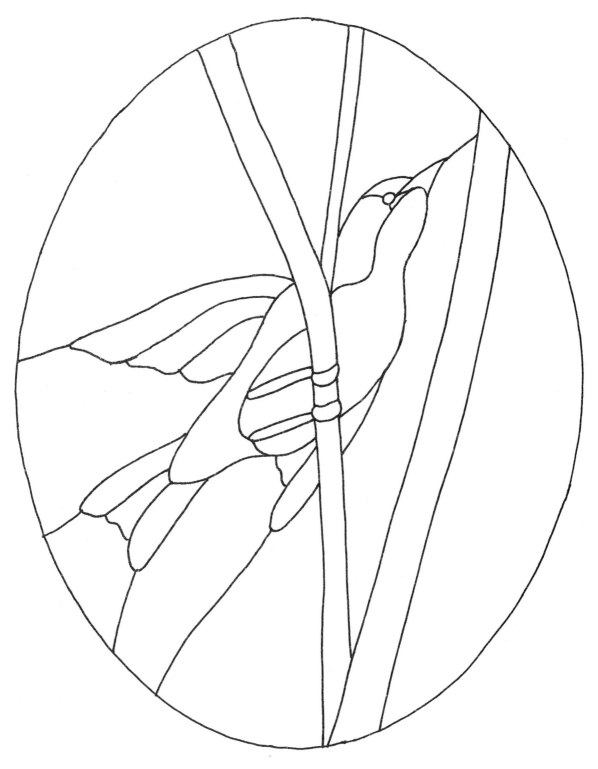

Northern Parula

(Female)

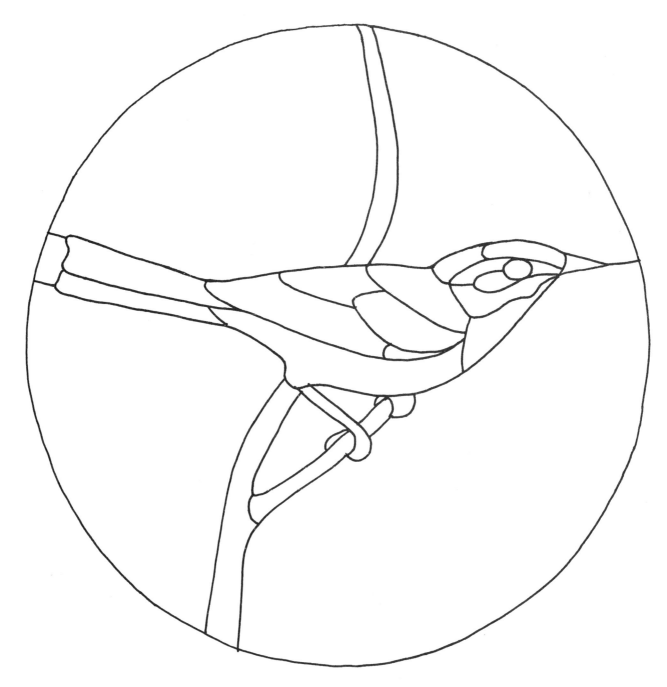

Golden-winged Warbler
(Male)

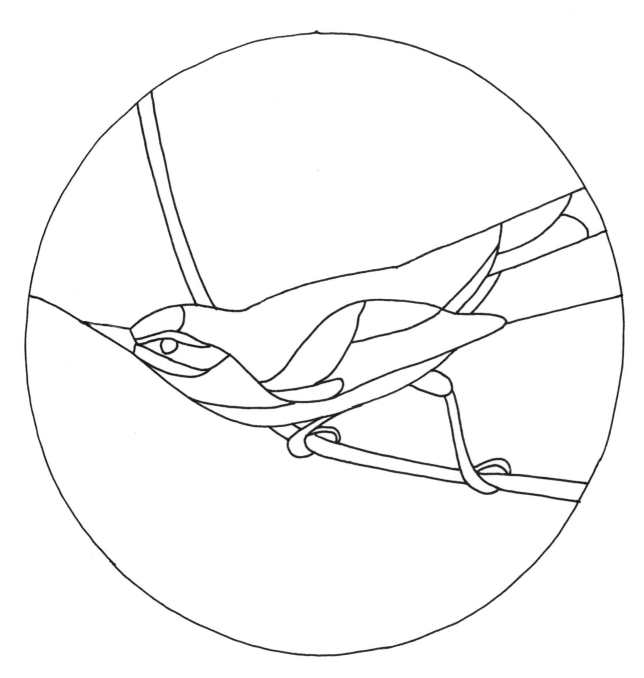

Golden-winged Warbler
(Female)

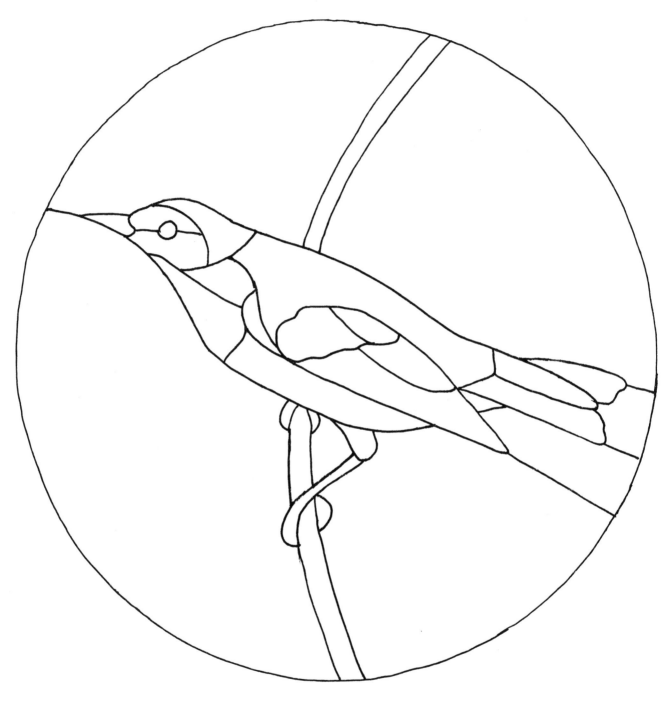

Bachman's Warbler

(Male)

Bachman's Warbler
(Female)

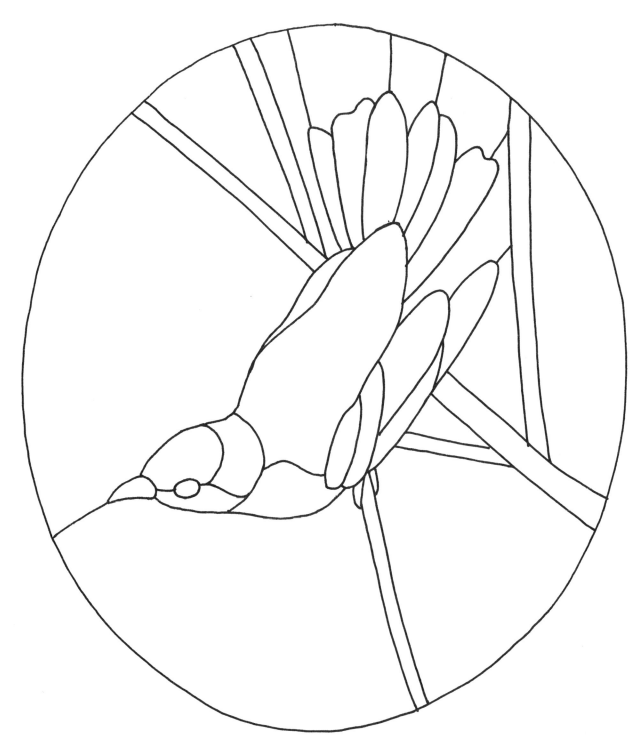

Blue-winged Warbler

(Male)

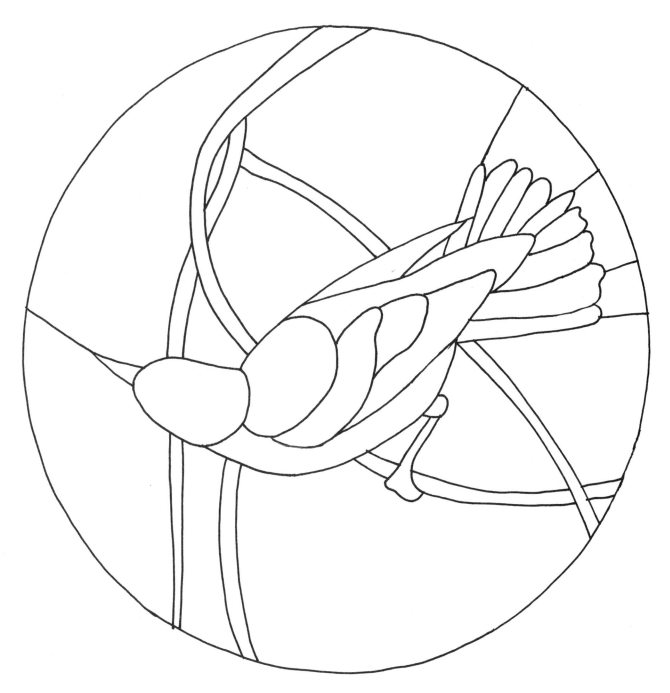

Prothonotary Warbler
(Male)

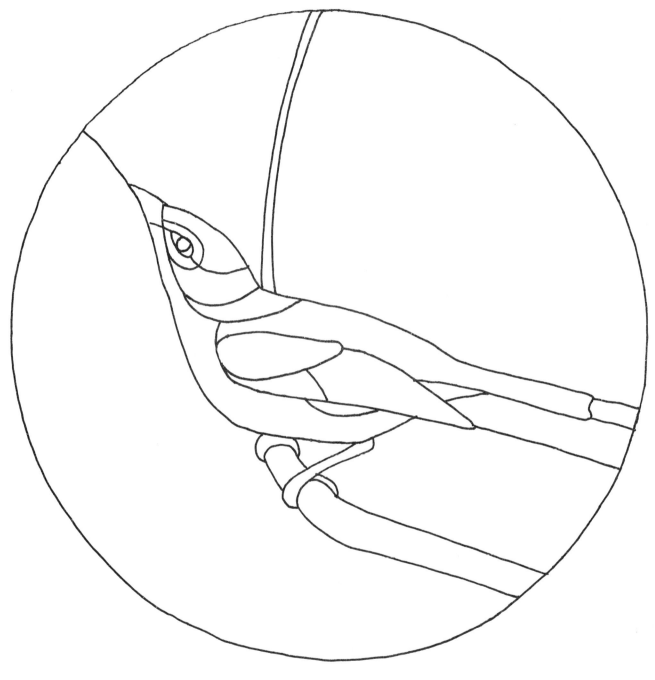

Warbling Vireo
(Male)

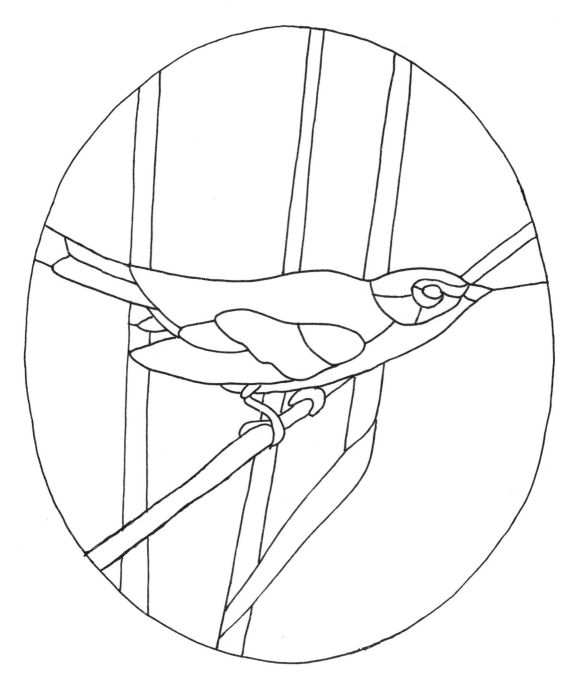

Solitary Vireo

(Male)

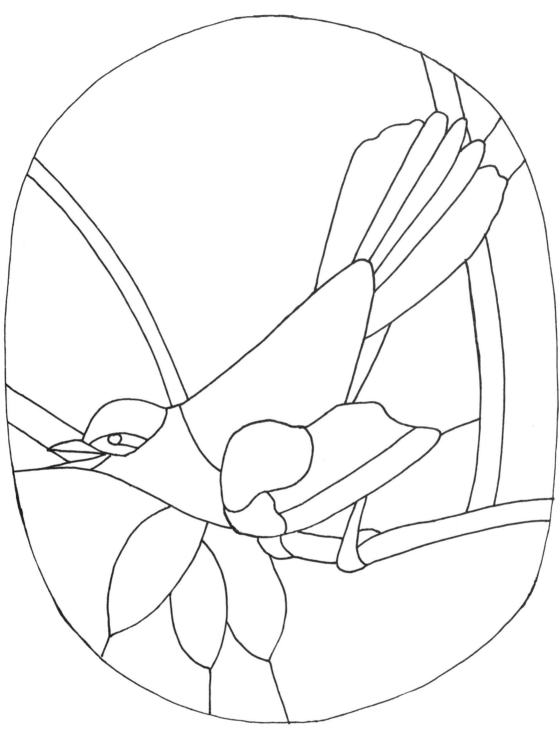

Gray Catbird

(*Male*)

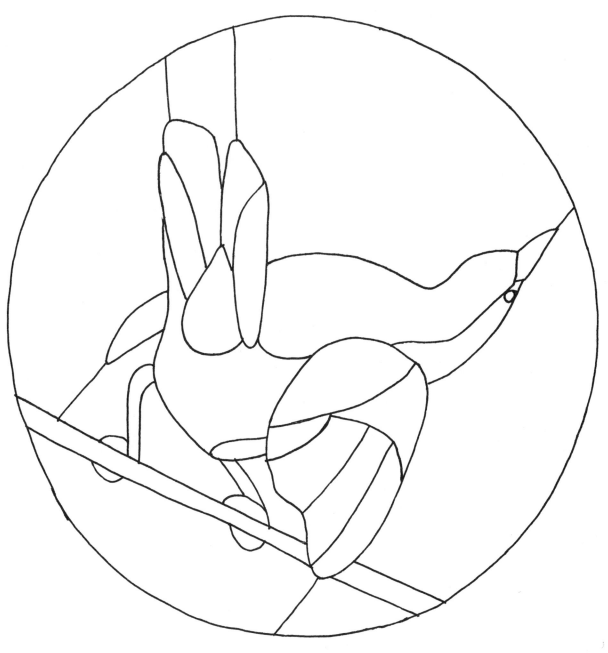

Gray Catbird
(Female)

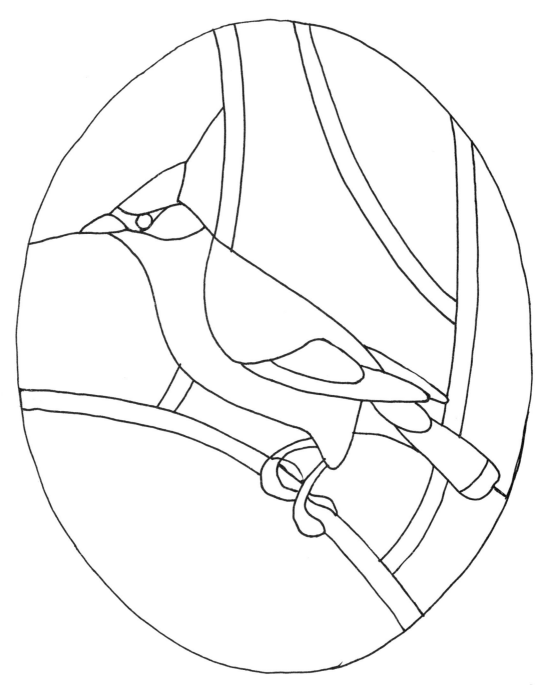

Cedar Waxwing

(Male)

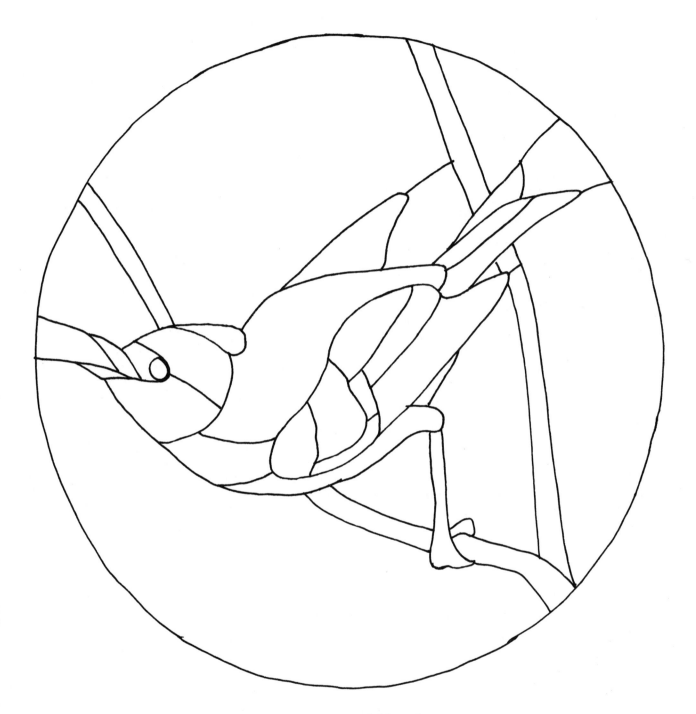

Ruby-crowned Kinglet
(Female)

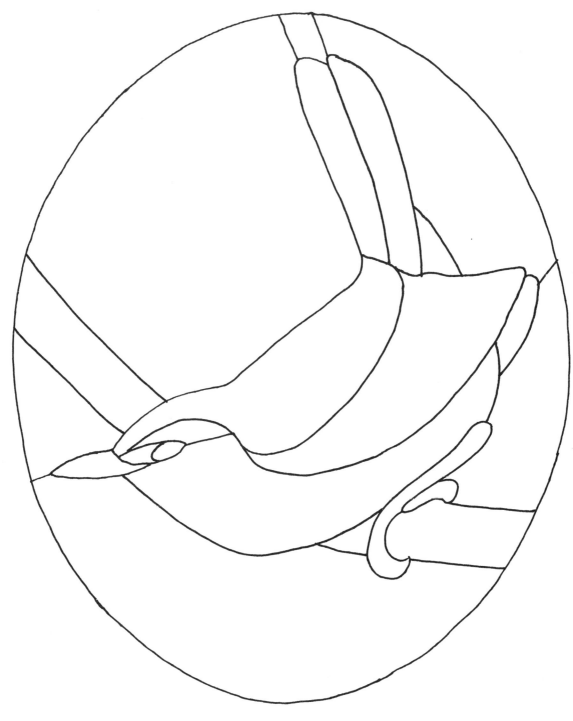

House Wren

(Male)

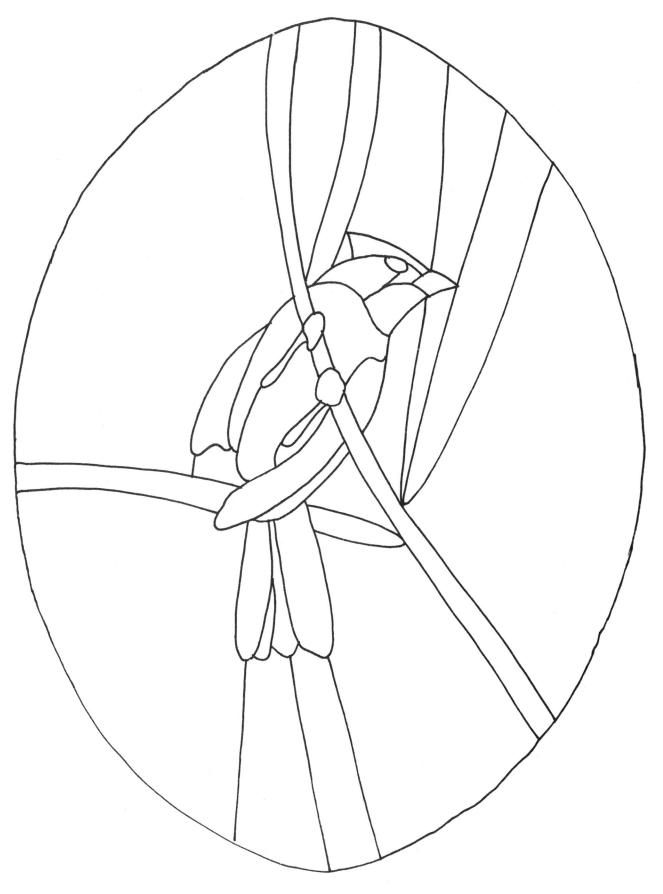

Tufted Titmouse

(Female)

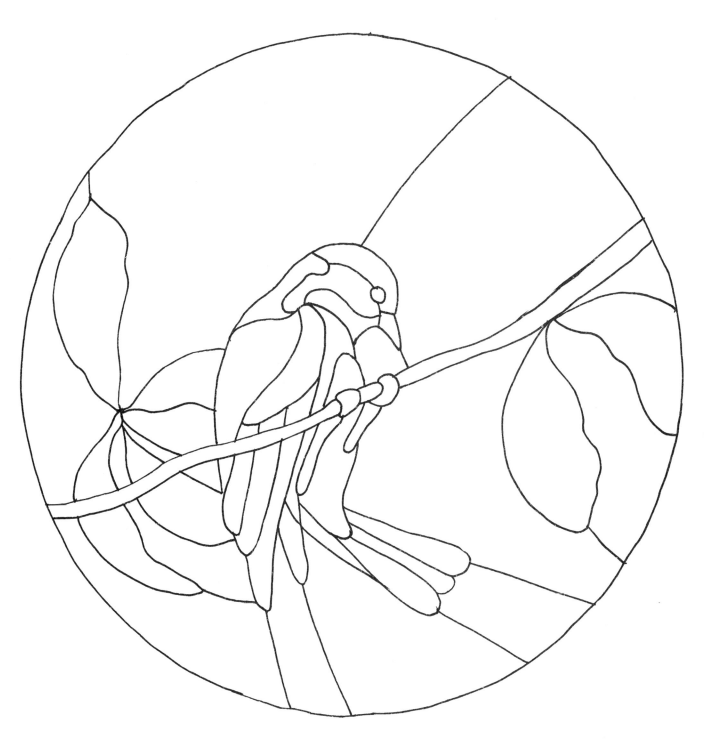

Chestnut-backed Chickadee
(Male)

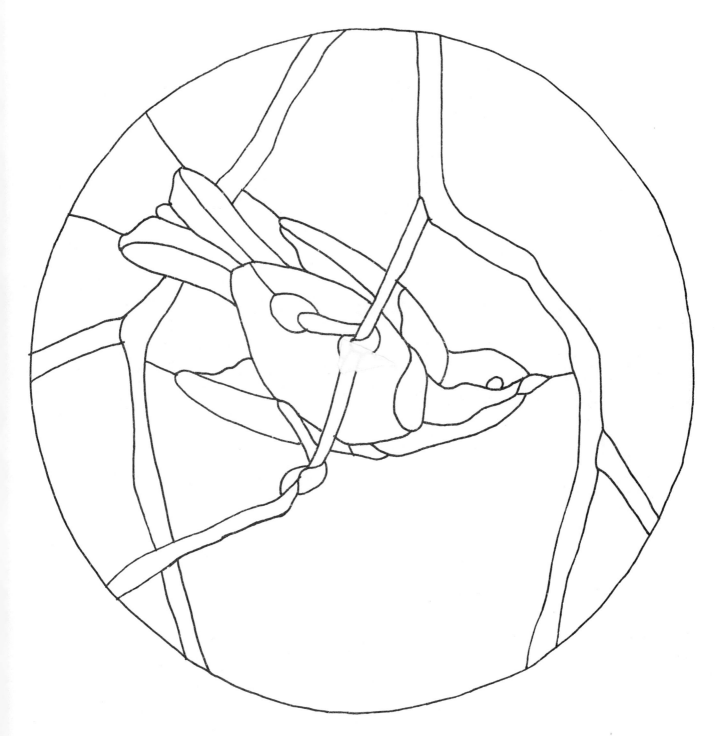

Chestnut-backed Chickadee
(Female)

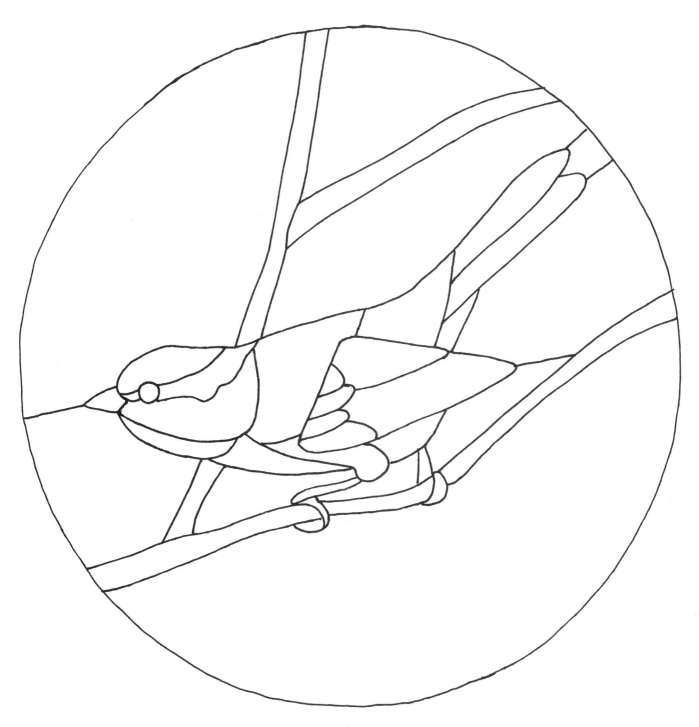

Black-capped Chickadee

(Male)